The ABCs of Baby #2

Surviving the Second Child One Letter at a Time

Written by
Kimberly Crabb
&
April Paine

Graphics by
Stephen Ashworth

A B C D E F G H I J

Q R S T U V W X Y Z

Dear Fellow Mom,

By now you've already heard, "If you think one is hard, just wait until you have two," or "Double the kids is double the work." These are the same well-meaning people who told you during your first pregnancy, "Boy, is your life going to change when you have a baby!" (As if you didn't know adding another human being to your family would change things?!)

We see the addition of the second child a little differently than your nosy neighbor: Your new arrival is nothing less than an adventure! Come along with us as we share all of the *helpful* advice we've gathered during our own parenting journeys.

After all, we've been there. We are two mothers of two, who also happen to be sisters (just 17 months apart) and best friends. We're not experts (and neither was our mother), but we've been in the trenches and have plenty of friends who have been, too. While we can't change the diapers for you or clean up the baby powder that your first born decided to sprinkle across the living room floor, we can offer support, and the best tips from moms who've seen it all before.

So now is your chance to do what you've always wanted to do: ignore the unhelpful advice from the lady on the street —and make a mental note never to say the same thing to another mom-to-be!

We'd love to hear from you! Catch up with us at ABCs of Family.com where we post ideas, tips and fun projects. If you have a suggestion for a mom-to-be, please share it with us. If we can use your original quote, you could end up as a Quotable Mom in the next edition of this book.

Hope to see you at www.abcsoffamily.com sometime soon.

With best wishes and congratulations,

Kimberly (the first born) & April (the baby)

A is for Adventure

Welcome to your big adventure! Yes, having a second baby *is* an adventure. And, like all adventures, it has its ups and its downs: it's exhilarating and exhausting; exciting and nerve-racking—but it's never dull. Most of all, it's a chance to open your hearts to another family member, and to help your first child learn how to open her heart, too.

A second baby is a chance to...

- ***Get real.*** Many first-time parents get lost in the fantasy of what parenting *should* be. By now you know the reality of what parenting *is:* hard work, fun, hard work, exciting, hard work, magical, hard work, amazing—and did we mention hard work? With Baby #2, you've already got a lot of this child-rearing stuff down. You know that you can't leave the house without a 20-pound diaper bag. You know that you *can* function on virtually no sleep. You know that the dry cleaner can get spit up out of your silk blouse. And, most importantly, you know that it all gets easier with time.

- ***Do it differently the second time.*** A second baby is a second chance—not to do everything "right," but to feel and enjoy the experience, and try new things. You may have had strict rules for your first child...you never let him sleep in your bed, watch TV during meals or skip a bath. The great thing about having another child is you get to make new choices and be a little easier on yourself. You've probably realized that you can break a few rules, and still have a happy, well-adjusted child.

"I was very uptight with my first child – I always kept him to a strict schedule and worried that any mistake I made would scar him for life! When I had my second baby 16 months later, I was much more relaxed and enjoyed the experience a lot more." Laura, mom of Noah and Gwyneth

BBBBBBBBBB

B is for Babies!

So your older child knows all about babies because she has a favorite doll or points to babies at the mall? Not so fast. Bringing a real, live, crying, pooping baby into your house will bring with it a whole new definition of "baby." You can help your first born get a more accurate idea of "baby" by introducing babies in the months preceding your new arrival.

Some things to try:

- ***Baby Play Dates***. If you're lucky enough to have a circle of friends where babies are abundant, make dates to visit with them. Your sibling-to-be will get to see, touch and entertain a real baby.

- ***Holding and Hugging***. With joy (and a big smile), let your child see you holding and hugging other people's babies and/or toy dolls. Include your child in the embrace.

- ***Play with Dolls***. Take your child to the toy store and let her choose her very own baby doll who will sit at the table with you when you have dinner, go for walks with you and ride in the car. Engage your first born by asking him what he thinks the baby doll would like for a drink.

- ***Diaper changing practice***. Buy extra diapers for your child to use with her doll.

- ***Make Sonograms a Family Affair***. Bring your child along to your sonograms. The photo may seem like nothing more than a moving blob, but the experience of going to the doctor's office or hospital for a sonogram will allow your child to think about what's to come.

- ***No Interest? Don't Sweat It.*** Some children have no interest whatsoever in babies—and that's fine too. Continue to talk about them and introduce your child to babies when you have the chance, but don't be concerned if babies aren't their thing.

"We borrowed a doll and stroller from friends and practiced how he might handle a baby. We taught him 'tickle the toes, tickle the toes' so he would only touch there." Kristen, mom of Will and James

C is for Catchphrases

The sibling-to-be will need to be told more than once about the baby's arrival and the baby's needs. Sometimes you just need a mantra to say over and over again to your older child. (Similar to the mantra you say to yourself: "This gets easier every day. This gets easier every day. This gets ..."). Keep your phrasing simple and consistent, and eventually, your first born will begin to get the idea.

Before the birth:

- You're going to be a big sister. What a super big sister you'll be!
- You're going to be very helpful with the baby.
- Mommy loves her big boy.
- Look at all the things big boys can do!

When Baby arrives home:

- Baby loves it when you talk to her.
- Baby loves it when you touch her toes.
- Baby thinks it's funny when you dance and jump.
- Baby says that you are a wonderful big sister.
- Do you remember being that small?
- You're such a caring big brother.
- Yes, you can use that toy, Baby loves to share.
- You're so sweet to Baby. She's lucky to have a big brother like you.
- Quiet words for tiny babies.
- Baby has to wait to play that game, but you're big enough.

"Whenever we spoke about the upcoming arrival and even once my youngest son was born, we always used the phrase 'our baby' This helped my older son feel like it was his baby too." Holly, mom of Gabe and Zack

D is for Dad

This is Dad's time to be a shining star! With the arrival of the second baby, Dad can take center stage. Now that the ratio has changed and the work has doubled (and redoubled), hard-working Dad can do what he does best: get things done.

- ***Stability.*** Mom's role has changed, but Dad is still pretty much the same. Since there are certain things only Mom can do right now (like nursing), Dad can fill the void and be there for the first born.

- ***Extra Time.*** The older child will delight in more attention from Daddy. Why not have a Daddy Fun Night? Once a week, Dad can take the older child out to dinner or an activity.

- ***Right-hand Man***. Dad can be there for Mom when she needs him most. But remember, your husband can't read your mind. Tell him what you need him to do. Write it down and tell him again. This isn't nagging. This is making sure that both parents of two small children are on the same page. And, yes, you need to be on the same page!

- ***Thank You, Honey.*** Although your husband may still not fold the towels the way you do, he'll love to hear you're grateful for his help. You love it when he appreciates you, so why not tell Dad how well he's doing? .

"When there are children in the house, it is impossible to have the time to think of someone else's perspective. My husband and I had to talk a lot about what was happening and what we needed from each other. I decided not to criticize how my husband took care of our kids. He found his comfort zone and I wanted that more than I wanted the kids' clothes to match, their hair to be combed or the counter to be cleaned off!" Alissa, mom of Ian and Cameron

E is for Encounter

Many parents dream of the moment that their older child meets the new baby. The first born will be ecstatic at the sight of his new sibling! The baby might even open his eyes when she hears the voice of the boy she can now call "brother." In reality, the baby undoubtedly sleeps or cries through the first encounter while the older sibling acts like a mutant has just invaded his house. A new puppy would have brought more delight. To get closer to your desired results, don't push. Remember that your darling duo has plenty of time to bond.

- ***Prepare.*** The need to prepare your older sibling can't be overstated. Long before Mom goes into labor, you must prepare your child with the facts: "Mommy is going to go to the hospital. Mommy is going to be away for a few sleeps but then Mommy will be back." And then you must go over those facts again and again. No matter the age of your first born, explanation and reassurance are vital.

- ***Have Grandma hold the baby***. When your older child sees you for the first time, it's important that someone else is holding the newborn baby. While you may feel you want to show one precious child to another, your first born will feel less threatened if Mom's arms are open for him right away. Ask Grandma or a nurse or, if no one else is available, Dad to hold the baby while you hug your older child.

- ***Gift* from *Baby*.** The proven way of gaining acceptance from a child: gifts! You can choose something small that can be handed over as soon as the two children meet. You don't need to spend a lot of money, but you should make an effort to choose something that will impress your older child - the next book in a favorite series, an addition to a doll house or train set, or a new DVD.

- ***Gift* for *Baby.*** Your older child will feel a sense of purpose when handing over a present he chose for the new baby. Don't micro-manage the choosing of the gift too much. If your older child wants the new baby to have a coloring book, then so be it. Choosing the gift, talking about the upcoming arrival and sharing special time with the older child is what's important.

"When we brought my baby daughter home, we had a 'Happy Big Sister Day' party (like a birthday party) for our older daughter. We had a cake and decorated the front door with signs for BOTH girls. My older daughter thought it was really cool! That way, it wasn't all about 'Welcome Home Baby.' My first child felt equally as important as the newborn baby!" Sheila, mom of Gabriella and Tori

FFFFFFFFFF

F is for Food

. . or picnic time! Get ready to eat on the floor—and probably *off* the floor, too! A picnic makes mealtime special. Both of your children need to eat, but your older child might not understand why Baby gets to be so close to Mommy, while she has to sit in a chair by herself. A picnic is one way to make ordinary daily tasks a little more fun, while helping you out. This isn't a big production, just grab a blanket and let your older child eat on the floor!

- ***Easy supplies to make it fun:***
    - Picnic basket (any basket will do)
    - Tablecloth (or blanket)
    - Paper plates, napkins (or a roll of paper towels) and utensils

- ***Turn on the TV.*** If you need a few peaceful moments, sitting your child in front of the TV for her picnic dinner won't ruin her for life. Why not buy a few new DVDs just for picnic time?

- ***Turn off the TV.*** Put on one of those perky kid's CDs—or one of your own—and let your older child have a picnic with her baby dolls and "friends."

- ***Choices, choices, choices!*** Let your older child choose the music, TV show, blanket, plates, etc.

"If my daughter ever wanted a cookie, I made her sit down to eat it. When her twin brothers came along, they followed my daughter's example. Now when I see them lined up in front of the TV, eating cookies and drinking juice, I'm so happy to have a moment's peace – and I'm so glad they have each other." Nicola, mom of Maddison, Brandon and Harvey

G is for Guilt

If you're a parent, you've already experienced guilt. It seems inevitable. When you have two, sometimes that means double the guilt. You feel guilty about your older child…What are you doing to your little best friend? Are you taking away his mommy time? Is he simply going to become a helper to you with the new baby?

If that's not enough, you feel guilty about your new baby…Your new little person will have to be toted all around, regardless of her nap schedule. You can't devote 24/7 to reading every book on sleep, poop and pre-pre-pre-college preparation like you did for your first. You can't help but wonder that maybe you weren't really ready to have Baby #2 so soon?

Some things to remember to ease your guilt:

- ***Time enough for everyone.*** Remember that when your older child starts school, you'll have a special time with your younger child.

- ***Time to share.*** This is a chance for your older child to learn to share—her space, your attention, her toys. That's not such a bad thing. It will help her later when she's in school and beyond.

- ***Time for flexibility.*** This is also a chance for all of you to learn how to be flexible—including the new baby. So what if he naps in the car seat as you run your older child to soccer practice? Most mothers of two will tell you that their second child is nothing if not flexible. They learn to go with the flow, and that's not such a bad thing. And the rest of your family learns to be flexible, too.

- ***Feel it and move on.*** Every new parent feels guilty at some point. But feeling guilty doesn't mean you *are* guilty. Just recognize that you feel that way, and move on.

"When we first brought my newborn son home, I felt guilty about showing him too much affection in front of my little girl. I tempered my adoration for my baby because I was afraid of how my daughter would react. But then I realized that she would actually learn how to love her brother – and so much more – by watching me love him. Instead of giving in to the guilt, I relished the chance to watch her love for him grow as I feel head over heels in love with him." Danna, mom of Lahna and Liam

H is for Help

Yes, yes, of course you won't need help—you can do it all by yourself, right? Wrong. You'll need help—lots of it. Childcare, meals, housework…you name it, you'll need it.

This isn't the time for the martyr act! No one doubts your abilities, but the simple fact is there's no need to do it all yourself. Two kids means double the work and double the exhaustion.

Don't be afraid to ask for help…

- ***From the grandparents.*** If you have doting parents or in-laws who can help with your baby or older child—great! Cherish the opportunity to have Grandma play a vital role. Whether she was gloriously helpful with your first baby or more laid back, she can now step in and help corral your two kids. Don't forget Grandpa—he might just surprise you!

- ***From a professional.*** Eventually family members have to return to their own lives, so hire a sitter or housekeeper to make things easier. A regular and consistent form of help will make the transition easier for everyone. As much as you want to do it all on your own, you'll be a happier person—and a better mother—if you get help so you don't feel overwhelmed.

- ***From a friend.*** If people offer to make meals or watch your older child, let them. You may think that they don't *really* want to watch another child (since you don't at this moment) but people like to feel useful. They've probably been in your place, and know how hard the first weeks (and months) are and want to help. In your former life, when you had sleep and time, you delighted in reaching out to friends. It's your turn to accept some kindness.

"Before our second child was born, a friend suggested we put money aside for babysitting only. That way, whether I wanted to spend time with my older daughter or get myself to a doctor's appointment on time, I was able to do it without worrying. I saw this as a wise investment in the well-being of my family." Jill, mom of Samantha and Tessa

I is for Idiotic Comments

Even the most helpful friends can slip up from time to time and feed you a line that makes your hair stand on end. Unfortunately, parents can be a wee bit competitive over their precious pups, and when you're exhausted from lack of sleep, hearing how perfect their little ones are can be irritating at best.

When you hear one of the following lines, just take a breath. (Since hitting other adults isn't acceptable, what else can you do?)

- "We never had *that* problem."
- "My older child didn't know the difference after a couple of weeks with the newborn."
- "My older child wasn't jealous."
- "My two children never fight."
- "My kids entertain each other for hours."

If someone you know is lucky enough to have two children who never argue and clean up their toys without being asked, then kudos to them! But don't doubt yourself or your energetic children. Besides, people should learn to save the bragging for grandma!

"People told me that my son and daughter would keep each other amused. This was very true…for a few minutes…until they'd get into a fight. Then nobody was laughing." Alyson, mom of DJ and Madison

J is for Jealousy

Many second-time parents worry about whether or not their first born will be jealous of the new baby. Spoiler alert: your older child *will* be jealous of the new baby. Imagine that your husband brings home another woman. He declares that he's madly in love with her, he wants you all to live together and, oh yeah, he wants you to love her too. How would you feel? We're guessing "joyful" doesn't come to mind. So how do you think your first child will feel when you bring home a new baby?

The good news is that you can lessen the jealousy by taking action to make your first child feel secure and well-loved.

- ***Reassure your first child.*** Say the words they cannot say. Articulate for them how they must be feeling about this life change and reassure them that you still love them more than anything.

- ***Create one-on-one time with mom.*** Even if it's lunch together while the baby sleeps, give your older child time with Mom and only Mom.

- ***Put your older child on Dad's schedule.*** Whether it's stories before bedtime or a regular Saturday breakfast at the local diner, make sure that your older child knows he's on Dad's schedule.

- ***Go back to the old days.*** Although it's logistically harder to organize, ask Grandma to look after your newborn for an hour while the Original Three – mom, dad and the well-adjusted older sibling—take a walk or play at the park.

"We dealt with my older daughter's jealousy by getting her involved in the care of her baby brother. We gave her age-appropriate jobs so she didn't feel left out. Whether she was in charge of bringing the diapers to me or drawing pictures for the baby, she was always given the opportunity to take part." Liz, mom of Megan and Clayton

K is for Kid Activities

Entertain *two* children? If this thought sends you running to the circus to hire a full-time clown, you're not alone. But the good news is, you don't have to. Your baby doesn't need to be entertained. She's happy to be snuggly in a car seat or leaning on your shoulder, while the other one plays.

A few ideas to keep the older one occupied:

- ***School days.*** This can be a great time to start Mother's Day Out or preschool. Think that's just a way to push your older child out the door? Think of it instead as a chance for your older child to be around friends, play outside, make messy projects and have a special place of his own.

- ***Two's company.*** There are lots of options for classes and programs with two children. Multi-age classes are a great way to do an activity as a family. This is not about getting your baby a head start, it's a way for your older child to get out and play while you bring the baby along. Check out gymnastics classes like Gymboree or music classes for mixed ages like Kindermusik or Music Together.

- ***Don't rush it.*** Start when you're comfortable. If two kids at the park is too much right now, get a sitter for the baby, so that you can have a special time with your older child.

- ***Get creative.*** Take your older child out for breakfast once a week before starting errands. Have dinner at the supermarket and then go grocery shopping.

"Last summer, I organized a week of activities for my two kids – including visiting the local children's museum, playing at a nearby park and having lunch at a fun restaurant. I then emailed my friends with the 'event list' and invited everyone to come along to any day that suited them. It was a great way to meet up with people without any hassle." Shannon, mom of Ella and Cooper

L is for Letting Go

This is no time for high standards. You don't need to remember your neighbor's cousin's birthday, send thank you notes within two days, make homemade cookies for the church bake sale and keep your house spotless. It's time to let go of your strong desire for perfection.

- ***Life with children isn't perfect.*** Now that you have more than one child, it's time to accept that your life (for the moment) is not going to run like it previously did. That's okay! Little people cause big changes. Let go of the need for perfection - and have fun with the chaos of family.

- ***Take your time with "Thank You" notes.*** People will forgive anything when you have a baby. Use this rare Mommy Pass to delay writing until you have time to do it. You may be thinking that you'll never have time (ever again), but ease the pressure by sending a quick email, make a phone call or have Dad send an e-greeting card.

- ***Food prepared in the microwave is still food.*** In the first weeks and months of life with two children, you'll need to cut corners and applaud yourself for feeding your family even if it comes in the form of a KFC bucket or a processed sandwich box that you once swore you'd never feed your child. Don't sweat it. This is a time to cut corners to save yourself some sanity.

- ***This is just a short time.*** You have eighteen years to show your new baby how tidy you keep your house and how good you are at making homemade apple pie. This is time for you and your family to enjoy snuggles, share laughs and get to know each other.

"When people ask me how I keep my house clean while still looking after my two young daughters, I tell them that my house isn't clean! I'd rather be playing house than cleaning house." Marty, mom of Kimberly and April

M is for Marriage

Two words: Date night.

That's it! We could fill this card with tricks and suggestions for a great marriage - but we have just one suggestion that will go further in helping your relationship than any 12-step program: a night out alone.

Date night is a chance to…

- ***Escape.*** Date night is a chance for you and your spouse to leave behind the house, the phone, the laundry, the bills and even those precious children. Even if it's for two hours once a week, it's an escape that can do wonders for all of you.

- ***Talk.*** Date night gives you a chance to talk face to face without being interrupted every 30 seconds by a crying baby, a dirty diaper, a broken toy, spilled juice or your older child's interpretive dance to Barney. Even if you spend a part of your night out talking about your kids, at least you're talking *about* them, and not *to* them—and you get to have a glass of wine while you do it.

- ***Put Your Marriage First.*** Going out alone with your husband reminds you that you're more than just parents—you're a couple who fell in love with each other long before the other loves of your lives came along. Best of all, you teach your children how important it is to have a marriage that's about more than who changes the next dirty diaper.

"You have to be really creative to have a date night sometimes. I set up our own evening out outside on the patio. I light candles, make a really nice dinner – and we have a little date. We're alone, the kids are asleep and we're doing something fun. Obviously, you have to make time for the date – and it's sometimes stressful getting to the part where you walk outside and enjoy the dinner – but once it's done, it's a great thing." Michelle, mom of Taylor and Andrew

N is for Nursing (or Bottle Feeding)

Remember when you would sit quietly in a dimly lit room with quiet music to feed your first born? Maybe you would read a book after the baby fell asleep on your chest or take a little nap yourself. How things change. Feeding Baby #2 can feel more like a juggling act than quiet bonding time. But the fact is, you'll still need time with the new baby where you can sit and feed rather than play action games with your older child.

Here are some strategies for making feeding time more relaxing for everyone:

- ***Warning***: Give the older child a warning. "In ten minutes, it will be time to feed your baby sister." "I think your baby sister is getting hungry. Let's read a story and then we'll feed her."

- ***Include:*** Ask the older child to choose a pillow or cushions for your back. Let him choose a blanket for the baby. Ask if he would like to read a book to the baby and keep you company during feeding time. Have a drink ready for your older child so he doesn't feel left out.

- ***Choices:*** "Do you want to sit on the couch with me while I feed the baby?" "Would you like to read Thomas or Elmo while I feed the baby?"

- ***Special toys*:** Have a basket of toys or books for your older child just for feeding time.

- ***Turn on the TV.*** Yes, the much maligned TV. Burn this card right now if you have to, but the TV can be helpful. Of course children shouldn't watch 12 hours of TV each day, but a short program can entertain your older child while you get on with the important work of nourishing a newborn.

"Feeding time became one of my family's best activities. My daughter would choose a book and then my baby son would 'pick' one too. It's been a great way to spend time together, reinforce sharing and start a tradition of reading." Cristina, mom of Lauren and Jason

O is For Organization

Having a newborn is not the time to get organized, but there are a few small things you can do to make your life feel more in control:

- ***Take the guess-work out of dressing.*** Pick clothes out the night before for you and your children. This eliminates frantic mornings standing in front of the closet in a fashion fog.

- ***Create an emergency kit for the car.*** It's too easy to be out and about without the things that you and your children need most. Although you may already feel that your diaper bag has enough items to stock a pre-school, it's a good idea to have a plastic supply box in your car with…
  - Diapers and Wipes
  - Change of clothes
  - Packaged snacks
  - Juice boxes
  - Bottles of water
  - Washcloths or Paper towels

- ***Reduce paperwork piles.***
  - Create a file with each child's name.
  - Keep in the kitchen or mudroom.
  - Place important papers (and fine art drawings) here until you have time to file appropriately.

"For me, it's all about pre-planning. Whether you're a morning person or a night owl, set time aside at one end of the day or another to pack lunches, lay out clothes, get things done. Don't wait to do what you need to do – inevitably, someone will spit up or have a poopy diaper (or both) just as you're trying to get organized." Julie, mom of Hallie, Jack and Kendall

P is for Pause

If all else fails, stop, breathe and do nothing.

Remember, this is not the time for…

- Potty training your older child
- Switching your older child from a crib to a toddler bed
- Changing routines
- Deciding that your older child WILL eat broccoli
- Losing weight
- Reading fashion magazines with pictures of skinny models
- New projects in the home, school or community-at-large. You can save the world next year!

"I started potty training my older son before his brother was born. After the baby arrived, I put a hold on it for about six months. The first several months were overwhelming, so I paused, and then potty training was really easy. I wanted everything to be perfect before my second son was born, but deciding to hold off was a better idea."
Lettie, mom of Hudson and Harrison

Q is for Quotable Moms

When you need good advice for those tricky parenting dilemmas, it's always a smart idea to ask a fellow mom. None of us have all of the answers, but all of us have some.

On being a parent today:
"Remember that our moms' generation was way more relaxed than we are about being moms – less stressed, less competitive, enjoying the moment more – and we all turned out so great. Relax and have fun with those babies!" Kristen, mom of Will and James

On family dynamics:
"We look at everything as belonging to the family…toys, food, books, movies. We put away all of our grown-up possessions so that the atmosphere is more laid-back. If the baby touched something – even if he touched one of my older son's toys--it was okay because all of us could. If my older son wanted something that the baby was holding, he had to bring the baby something else. He wasn't forbidden from taking it, he just had to help the baby because the baby couldn't do it on his own. Ian is still really good at helping his friends and not being too possessive of things." Alissa, mom of Ian and Cameron

On siblings close in age:
"My boys are 22 months apart. At first, the age difference is a little challenging…double diaper duty, double baby/toddler proofing, etc. but now my boys are 8 and 6 and the age difference couldn't be better. They play well together and get along great (most of the time!)" Amy, Mom of Rylan and Hudson

On keeping routines:
"Because my husband travels a lot, we have a strict routine in place for the boys. That way, we're all on the same page. When my husband comes home, he takes over and gives me a break while our children continue with the same schedule – often without us having to say anything!" Edye, mom of Adam and Ryan

On work and family:
"With a full-time job and children, I have to have a consistent schedule to keep our family running smoothly. Whether I'm the one putting my daughters to bed, or the nanny or the grandparents, we keep the same schedule so the girls know what to expect. This also means I know what to expect and how to plan each day." Collin, mom of Kira and Zooey

On keeping things fair:
"Ava was 21 months old when her brother was born, and she, of course, still needed lots of one-on-one attention. I found myself constantly saying, 'Just a minute, I need to take care of Owen.' So to make things more fair, I started asking Owen to wait as well. He would be sound asleep in his bouncy seat, but still I would say, 'Owen, it's Ava's turn so you wait right there.'" Liz, mom of Ava and Owen

On special time:
"I really treasured the last few months with my daughter before her younger brother was born. She was so special to me, and I felt guilty that this would be our last time with just the two of us, and that she would have to share my attention. Obviously, having another child has been joyful, but I still look forward to our special 'girl times.'" Barrie, mom of Alexandra and Caden

R is for Road Test

Older children will be keenly aware that the baby gets to do and have things that Big Boys and Girls don't--which means, they'll want it, too. We call this the "road test."

If your older child expresses an interest, go ahead and let her try out…

- Pacifiers
- Teethers - especially the ones that vibrate
- Baby Bathtub
- Baby Food
- Bottles
- Crib
- Blankets

Afraid all this means your big kid will revert and be in diapers again—not just for a little while, but for the *rest of her life*??? Don't worry. Baby items will lose their glamorous appeal very quickly if you don't make a big deal out of their use. Whether your first born is 16 months or 16 years, what he really wants is to be a Big Boy.

"My older daughter wanted to use all of the baby's things. You name it, she tried it. We didn't mind. She even found a way to fit in the tiniest Moses basket imaginable. When our little girl's friends came over for play dates, every child tried out our baby daughter's bouncy seat. One after another, they climbed in and had a great time." Lyn, mom of Kate and Beth

S is for Sanity

Nothing saves your sanity like the occasional bribe. Realize that your older child likes a special treat as much as you enjoy a nice pedicure, long massage or a big piece of chocolate. Why not indulge her every now and then? Your older child has gone from two doting parents to two zombie creatures and a crying alien in the next room—isn't a lollipop okay?

- ***Treats at hand***. If the new baby receives a gift in the mail or you need to distract your older child so that your newborn can latch on to feed, have a treat ready to share.

- ***Treats don't need to be sweet.*** Treats don't have to equal sugar and extra visits to the dentist. Your child wants to spend time with you more than anything in the world. He'd rather have a story on your lap than a cookie on his own. However, it's not a perfect world and sometimes the cookie gives you the chance to do what you need to do so that special time is possible later.

- ***It's not forever.*** Treats won't spoil your child permanently. Remind your older child that it's a special time when babies are born and children become big brothers or sisters. By repeating the "special time" concept to your older child (no matter how young), she'll begin to realize it's not permanent.

- ***Favorite treat ideas:***
  - Activities with Mom or Dad only
  - Party favor toys
  - Bubbles (no spill, sprays, scented, bubble machines)
  - Bath treats (fizzies, bath bombs, bath crayons)
  - Stickers
  - Juice boxes and small packages of cookies
  - Dollar aisle treats

"Getting two children into car seats was a nightmare. I put a bag of treats and a box of books in the car; whenever we got in, I offered them a well-timed distraction." Kimberly, mom of Jack and Reagan Lee

T is for talk to your child

Never think that your child is too young to understand that a sibling is on the way. While he may not understand the complexities of a changing family dynamic or the ongoing discussion about when Daddy plans to clean out the garage, your Little Person has more understanding than you might guess. Because we don't know for sure the moment that children "get it," wouldn't it be a shame to miss the opportunity to ease their fears?

- ***Before the birth.*** Tell your older child that he is going to have a baby brother or baby sister. Explain that things will be different, but new babies are exciting! Discuss the changes that will occur once the baby has arrived. The big brother or big sister needs to know what life with a baby will be like. Talk about all of this again tomorrow…and the next day.

- ***During the birth.*** You'll be slightly busy, so leave instructions with Grandma. Share the news that the baby is finally arriving. Ask the new sibling if he has any questions. Clarify the plans for Mom's hospital stay or expected time away.

- ***After the birth***. Talk *for* the baby. Tell the older child what the older baby is thinking and feeling. While you may feel silly translating the language of Baby for your older child, you play a vital role in helping your older child understand what this new little creature is going through.

"Once our twins were home from the hospital, it really helped our toddler when we would narrate all the changes that were occurring in her life. At two and a half, she didn't yet have the ability to fully process all of her conflicting feeling about being a big sister - the excitement of new babies, the fun of all the friends and family we had at the house helping out, the upset of losing Mommy and Daddy's focus and the exhaustion of managing all the additional stimulation. Talking her through all those changes and making sure that she understood that it was okay to feel both happy and sad seemed to help her get through the initial mayhem of bringing two newborns into our lives." Stacey, mom of Sadie, Ruby and Adelaide

U is for Understanding

The importance of having friends who can understand what you're going through is vital right now. You need to know that you're not alone.

- ***Find a friend***. Spend time with another mom in the same situation. Talking to someone with a new baby, even if it's their first, is a huge lifesaver.

- ***Make a play date***. Invite other moms to play at your house. We promise, their sink is full of dirty dishes, too.

- ***Join a Mom's group.*** Don't go it alone. Mom's groups can offer playtime for moms and their kids, or childcare while moms chat and connect. Online moms groups can be helpful too, but nothing replaces face-to-face contact.

- ***Be aware.*** Don't be surprised if friends with older children—even multiple children—aren't as supportive. They have long forgotten about mysterious rashes and midnight feedings. That's why having someone in the thick of things can help.

"My book group was a great source of understanding and support after having my second child. It was not only a nice break from motherhood duties, but most of my friends were in the same second baby boat." Carrie, mom of Tommy and Drew

V V V V V V V V V V

V is for Vacation

Vacationing with children is less like your honeymoon in the Caribbean and more like a change of scenery. But even a change of scenery can be fun, as long as you're ready for it.

- ***Get a Co-Captain.*** No matter how young your first child is, he'll love the idea of being your special helper on the journey. Explain what the travel will be like and enlist him to assist you on the way. Be sure to bring treats as Co-Captains can get hungry and bored.

- ***Send your stuff ahead of time.*** With two children, you'll have a lot to bring with you. Pack up a box of diapers, clothes and essentials to have waiting for you at your destination. If possible, book an online grocery delivery to arrive when you do.

- ***Time it right.*** Travel at a time that suits the older child's nap schedule or happiest time. The new baby will be content in a snugly car seat or mom's arms. Take advantage of the fact that newborns are portable.

- ***Alert the airlines!*** You've got two kids! While this may sound highly dramatic, it's always good to contact the airlines about any rules, restrictions or upgrades (you don't get it if you don't ask!). Different airlines have different policies, but you may be eligible for a sky cot bassinet, a kids' pack or a friendly smile at check-in.

"My husband and I took our baby daughter and toddler son on their first international flight during a short period of extreme heightened airline security. We weren't allowed to bring anything onboard with us – no baby toys, no toddler treats – not even my 2 year old's favorite teddy bear. We ended up sitting on the tarmac for four hours before departing on ten hours of in-flight misery. We didn't even have a box of crayons to write over and over, 'I will never fly with children again. I will never fly with children again.' *Although we weren't laughing at the time, we still enjoy traveling with the kids and remembering that crazy time we first flew as a foursome."*
April, mom of Robbie and Jessica Martha

W is for Wailing

W is also for whining, whoa is me, or what the heck have I done? There's no getting around the fact that crying is a part of early childhood. You can expect a lot of it—from your baby, from your older child and likely from yourself, too. As hard as it can be to listen to, remember that crying doesn't hurt anyone. Still, you can lessen it's disquieting impact...

- ***Discuss crying***. Many children feel nervous when a new baby cries. Eventually, they'll learn to tune the noise out (and even sleep through it), but in the beginning, it's good to explain that this is the only way the baby can communicate. Think of it this way, if it's uncomfortable, annoying and nerve-racking for you to hear the baby cry for more than five minutes—and you're the cognizant adult—of course it's normal that a small child would be upset.

- ***Remain Calm.*** The older sibling will model your behavior. If you are unaffected by the crying, then he will be too. The good news is that the cries of a baby are nothing compared to those of a toddler or teen, so you'll be amazed at how easy it is to remain composed while navigating a screaming baby and an interested sibling.

- ***Ease the pain.*** If your baby cries every car trip, don't be surprised if your older child squirms and fidgets when it's time to get into the car. Make it easier by having a special toy or book reserved especially for car trips.

Your older child's dinnertime is often prime wailing hours for the baby. If possible, get a friend or a sitter to take your baby for a walk during that time so your child can enjoy a quiet meal with you, instead of competing with a fussy baby.

- ***Enlist your Big Kid's Help.*** Ask your older child what she thinks would help the baby feel better—and take up her suggestion (even if it's dancing the limbo—after all, what could it hurt?). Maybe ask her to pick out a favorite CD to play or turn the water on in the bathroom if that soothes the baby.

"I wanted my daughter to know that her future brother would not be a lot of fun in the beginning. I told her that babies 'eat, sleep, poop and cry'. I would say, 'Waaahhhh!' and ask her, 'What is that?' She'd say, 'It's a baby.' I would ask her, 'What do babies do?' She would say, 'Waaahhhh!' This has really helped, and she's not phased by the crying, because she knows that's what babies do when they're little." Julie, mom of Jocelyn and Jacob

X is for Xtra Special Time

As hard as a second child may be, there's no denying the fact that it's a special time. Your family is growing. There's some peace in knowing that dinner, sleep and shopping will never be the same—and you don't care.

Remember to…

- ***Shoot it.*** Take a lot of photos. You'll be glad you did. And don't just capture the happy moments—capture those unhappy moments, too. Although you might not think you would ever want a picture of your baby screaming in the bouncy seat while your older child mopes on the couch, those moments are part of life, too—and it will remind you of how far you've come.

- ***Film it.*** Use the video camera. Capture the action movie of the year.

- ***Celebrate it.*** Don't spend the weekend doing chores. Get out there with your family and enjoy being together.

- ***Cherish it.*** Sometimes with all the hard work that goes into having two children, you forget about the unexpected joys of a little baby: the weight of their little body against your chest; the feathery hair; the first two weeks of "honeymoon" time when newborns sleep all the time; watching your older child kiss, hold, feed the baby; and that great newborn smell.

"As soon as our second son arrived, we were far more confident in what we could do with a baby. When he was just 5 months old, my husband, older son, the baby, and I all went to see a show at the theatre. We had a wonderful time. When you have your first child, it changes your life completely. Once the second arrives, your life is changed already so none of us felt we were missing out on anything. Having a second child allowed us to come together as a family."
Paula, mom of Eoin and Ned

Y is for You

Finding time for YOU is incredibly important; this is one of the most difficult tasks for Moms to accomplish, but we suggest that you put it on your "to do" list—along with all of the other jobs that keep your home and family running smoothly. So take time each day for yourself.

- ***Read.*** Grab a magazine. Save *War & Peace* for when your kids are in college. Now's the time to sit down for 10 minutes and let your thoughts wander from Hollywood gossip to someone else's home redecoration.

- ***Drink and chat.*** Enjoy a cup of coffee, or even a glass of wine. Make a phone call (to a friend, not the plumber).

- ***Submerge***. Take a bubble bath. You may be thinking that a bubble bath is a relaxation cliché, but there's a reason that this time-honored activity is always suggested. Give it a try. Even a quick dunk will revive you.

- ***Sit.*** Pray, meditate or listen to music. Do nothing but sit still and just *be* for a few minutes.

"You" time does *not* mean…
Cleaning cupboards, running errands, calling that new neighbor to see how she's settling in, folding clothes, cooking dinner, organizing school bags…anything that involves Mom at work rather than Mom at rest!

"I put both my kids in childcare at the local Y for an hour while I use the gym. It's great for my older son because he gets a chance to play with other children. While I was hesitant to put my baby daughter there too, I can see how well they care for her – and how she spends most of the time sleeping any way – so I take the opportunity to exercise so that I feel good. It's a win-win situation!" Catherine, mom of Dylan and Lauren

Z is for ZZZZZZZZZZZZZZZZ (as in sleep)

Okay, here's the good news—your newborn will usually sleep a lot the first few weeks after you bring him home. This is the honeymoon period and helps you get adjusted. But what about *after* those first few weeks? Selling your kids on eBay is not an option, so we'll suggest a few other things:

- ***Stick to a Schedule.*** Although we know how hard it is to get one child on a regular sleeping routine—much less two—the fact is, children thrive on structure and routine. It's important to create a livable schedule and stick to it. For the older child, write (or draw, if they can't read) a list of the bedtime routine and tape it to the bathroom door: bath, brush teeth, pajamas, book, nightlight, to bed. He'll thrive on the predictability of it. For the baby, it's never too early to start a bedtime routine that he'll begin to equate with sleep.

- ***But Don't Be a Slave to It.*** While schedules are important and, ultimately, make life easier, there are times when you have to let the schedule slide—especially if a kid is sick, or you're traveling, or you're just having a bad day. Do what you need to do to make it work. You can regroup later.

- ***Remember that Babies are Hearty Sleepers.*** Most babies could sleep through an Aerosmith concert. You might have kept the house as quiet as a tomb when your first born was sleeping, but that's not an option with Baby #2—and it doesn't have to be. While you may not want the older child to compose her first symphony while the baby is sleeping, let her do activities that make a reasonable amount of noise. After all, she can't be quiet all the time!

- ***Break the rules.*** A newborn creates chaos, there's no getting around it. Recognize this and break some of those steadfast sleep rules if it means getting a good night's sleep. You may do all the things with Baby #2 that you said you'd never do with your first child—like letting your older child sleep on a sleeping bag on the floor of your room if the baby is in there, too. Remind your older child that this is special and will only be for a few days.

- ***Make Your Older Child's Room Special.*** If you don't want your older child sleeping in your room, help make his room a little more special. Let him pick out a new special blanket or nightlight. Find a special stuffed animal to keep him company. Also, remember that what works for you may not work for your child. You may sleep in total darkness, but your child may need a light or the door cracked. Without going overboard, talk with your child and help him make his room as comfortable as possible.

- ***Do What Works for You.*** You can find many good sleep books out there, and even more good advice from friends, your mother and even mother-in-law—but ultimately, you have to do what works for you and your children.

- ***Take time.*** Give yourself a little more time to get comfortable with your growing family, your recovery and the newness of it all. Just when think you'll crash because of lack of sleep, your babies start sleeping better. We promise that you will survive!

"I used some sleep training methods to help my daughter sleep on her own from an early age. When her brother was born, that seemed to go out the window. All of the rules didn't seem to work anymore. Some nights she slept with us, my husband slept on the couch, or it was musical beds. It wasn't an ideal situation, but we did all sleep – and at that time in our lives, that's what was most important. This phase didn't last forever, and it gave us some much needed rest." Jenny, mom of Corley and Herd

ABCs of Family.com

Don't reinvent the wheel...
Just add some sparkle to the spokes!

We wish you all the best as you enjoy Baby #2!

Please visit us at abcsoffamily.com.

10573623R00033

Printed in Great Britain
by Amazon.co.uk, Ltd.,
Marston Gate.